Young Cupid!

Umbrelly Books Publishing
Est. 2006, Saratoga CA

- Young Cupid! -

No portion of this publication may be reproduced or transmitted, in any form or by any means, without the express written permission of the copyright holder. Names, characters, places and incidents featured in this publication are either the product of the author's imagination or are used fictitiously. Any resemblance to actual persons (living or dead), events, institutions, or locales, without satiric intent, is coincidental. For information regarding permissions, please contact:

Umbrelly Books – Children's Literature
PO Box 2 7 0 3
Saratoga, CA 95070

Copyright © 2008 Johnny DePalma
All rights reserved

For more information on this book
Please visit our website:

www.umbrellybooks.com

1 2 3 4 5 6 7 8 9 10

First Edition

Printed in the United States of America

ISBN 978-0-6152-0654-7

For Amanda

Once upon a time, you see,
while browsing books of destiny,

Young Cupid,

who was unemployed,

paused upon us,

overjoyed,

And shouted,
"I know what to do!
I'll fix up couples"
(Like me - like you)

He took an arrow
and a bow
And added glitter
just for show.

And practiced
with it every night
till raging passions would ignite.

And once the man had popped his cork, nine months later had come a stork.

But…
on went Cupid with caffeine
until the people,
like sardines
Were packed together so very tight
That all the people **began to fight.**

"Perhaps," Cupid began to say, "It's time to take a holiday.

And, you know, that's what I'll do! So see ya later and toodle-loo!"

And after that,
once love was gone
and starving artists
wrote sad, sad songs,

This population
had said Goodbye
And one by one
began to die.

For without love
there is no life
There is no husband
and no wife.

There
is no
air worth
breathing here.
Just empty time and
empty fear.

And Cupid realized
he was wrong
And that he *really*
did belong.

So…

with this new found admiration
he said, "I'll continue…
In moderation
And save my arrow
for true love only
Not every single
one who's lonely.

Yes, indeed, that's  what I'll do!"

And that's what he did
For me - For you

the end

ABOUT THE AUTHOR

Johnny began writing down his absurdities at a very early age; and, I should add - is most likely continuing to write them now. To date, Mr. DePalma has won several awards in the arts, ranging from his acting to his writing and back again. This is Mr. DePalma's third book.

About the Illustrator

Molly began illustrating many years ago in a
small Parisian bookshop; copying images from Alice in
Wonderland and A Tart's Progress. Back in New York, she
continues to create cheeky Victoriana for clients such as
The New York Times and The Wall Street Journal.